Embracing
the Spirit
of Nature

Linda Shaylor Cooper

Edited by Lane Badger and Ariela Wilcox
Illustrated by Katie Doka
Photography by Linda Shaylor Cooper, Phil Benson, Mary Zaranto and Nita Seneca

Balboa Press books may be ordered through booksellers or by contacting:

Balboa Press
A Division of Hay House
1663 Liberty Drive
Bloomington, IN 47403
www.balboapress.com
1-(877) 407-4847

ISBN: 978-1-4525-4031-3 (sc)

Library of Congress Control Number: 2011918802

Printed in the United States of America

Balboa Press rev. date: 11/17/2011

BALBOA PRESS
A DIVISION OF HAY HOUSE

Waking Up
to a
World
Filled with
Fairies

Written by Linda Shaylor Cooper
Edited by Lane Badger and Ariela Wilcox
Illustrated by Katie Doka
Book designed by David Davis/Chris Davis
Photography by Linda Shaylor Cooper,
Phil Benson, Mary Zaranto
and Nita Seneca

We are all familiar with Disney's Tinker Bell, Thumbelina, Peter Pan and other famous fairies and we might have seen the flower fairy books of famous British illustrator, Cicely Mary Barker, but do we ever stop to ask ourselves these questions:

Are we living in a world populated by these unseen beings?

And... could they actually be real?

The 'concept' of nature spirits, the fairies, and other beings of the devic kingdom, has been around since humans have been walking upon the Earth. Generally speaking, they have been relegated to the realms of mere fantasy. We have certainly read about them in books. We have seen drawings of them by people who say that they can see them. And there are plenty of movies on the subject, especially in the form of cartoons and movies for children. But for those who have never seen them with their physical eyes, there is the tendency to entirely dismiss the fairy world.

My personal experience has been to read every book that I could find on the subject of fairies as well as watch movies like A Midsummer Night's Dream, Peter Pan, and Fairie Tale — A True Story and most recently Avatar. When I was a young girl I wanted to believe that they existed, but I was never quite sure because I had never seen one. Delving into the realms of fantasy uplifted my emotional body bringing me to places of knowing that anything that I could imagine was possible.

In my early thirties I had the good fortune to meet a woman who became my spiritual teacher, sharing her knowledge of these unseen aspects of reality. She introduced me to a vast spectrum of information that I had no idea existed. One day I asked her the big question,

"Do fairies really exist?"

She looked me straight in the eye and answered, "Of course they do, my dear!"

She then got up from her chair and went directly into her library to access her books on the subject. She gifted me with a book called *A True Fairy Tale by Daphne Charters*. Daphne Charters (1910-1991) had a personal relationship with the fairies in her garden in England and they shared information about their lives, their work and their hierarchical structure. So far, it has been the best information I have ever experienced and the fairies themselves have assured me that it is the truth. So I will share some of her information in this book.

Mommy tulip supporting her baby on her back

I feel so much wonder and love for the fairies. As a landscape designer and builder for many years, I have been blessed with the opportunity to create many lovely gardens with the help of these beneficial nature spirits. The gardens we created together were filled with a shimmering light that was not apparent in the surrounding gardens. I can remember times where standing in front of a wide open rose being kissed by the sun brought me to tears with its beauty. Spending time in gardens with the Nature Spirits influence has taught me about being still. The plants, flowers and trees rooted in the ground with their faces reaching for the sun and expressing beauty is their job. Whenever I felt stressed stepping into the garden would calm my nerves. It has been, and still is, a pleasure and a gift for which I am deeply grateful. Truly it is a miracle that they have shown up in the photos of this book, making

their presence known for everyone. What a joy it has been to have experienced and discovered them.

"It was beyond my wildest dreams."

I gladly share my thoughts, experiences and the photographs in this book *Embracing the Spirit of Nature* with you, in the hopes that you too will see the nature spirits and feel the magic of earth's enchanted garden.

I have found out through sharing these photographs with friends that each person perceives something different. It has helped to expand my own awareness. When you revisit the photographs you will find images that you may not have noticed the first time around. The Nature Spirits have shown up sometimes as faces other times as winged beings or as animals. They seem to want us to see them with shapes that we can identify. Try looking at the photos from all angles. I am in constant awe at what is revealed each time I look at the pictures. Enjoy the magic with your heart and mind wide-open, and have fun while viewing what the fairies have revealed so that your imagination can embrace the new dimension of the Nature Spirits.

Author's Note to the Reader

My initial thoughts around creating this book were to express from my own experience and not research or present other people's work. However, I am so impressed with the information coming through Daphne Charter's work that I have decided to include some of her findings. Daphne Charter's writings have been currently re-visited in a book called "Forty Years with the Fairies" which I highly recommend for a more in depth education. In fact, I have asked the fairies themselves for permission to do so, and they have assured me that her information is accurate.

What I have chosen to do with some of the photos of the nature spirits that have been collected is to channel the beings themselves, asking them what they want to share with all of us. For me channeling is a process where I sit quietly, breathe deeply, call in protection and the support from my guidance, then ask for information that is clear and for the best and highest good of all concerned. Then I focus on the photo of the being in front of me asking and receiving dialog in my thought field then writing them down. Much of what I am sharing here has come from my own personal studies and experiences.

The raw photographs that you will view have been cropped, in some cases lightened and enlarged.

How I became a Garden Fairy

Ever since I was a small girl I have always been fascinated with the idea of the fairy realm and read every fairy story I could find. When life seemed overwhelming I would escape into my imaginary life in fairyland. I loved playing in the garden, hiding under the trees and bushes, feeling safe and secure imagining being surrounded by the fairies.

My parents were in the habit of moving frequently. We made a move from South Africa to America when I was eleven years old. I grew up, continuing my schooling in Southern California. In the back of my mind, I always wondered if fairies were real. I married in my mid-twenties to a man who practiced law and expected to have a normal life of home and children. He was not a husband who was happy to go to work. It soon became obvious to me that he really did not want the responsibility of children, as his work was highly stressful. After seven years with him I was ready to bail out of the marriage!

Instead of separating we agreed to go on an adventure. He took a sabbatical from his law practice so that we could spend one year traveling. Our goal was to travel to the tip of South America and back in our VW bus, which was outfitted with every imaginable item to ensure our survival. Mind you, camping was not in my comfort zone, but it was in his. So I trusted and we jumped off the edge together.

We could not get through El Salvador at that time, as it was involved in a war so we ended up spending four months in Mexico and three months in Guatemala, and the rest of the year in the western states of North America. As we were coming to the end of our journey we found ourselves wanting to do it again. I let him know that I was not spending another year in a VW bus so we purchased a 26-foot school bus with the idea to build it into a traveling home. Upon our return home, my husband gave up his law practice and got a job as an RV mechanic so that we could build our bus to take our next adventure. It took us two and one half years to complete the bus, which turned out beautifully.

Organized religion was not a part of either of our lives. Upon our return from our first trip it dawned upon me that there must be more to life than the pursuit of the financial and material quest. When I awoke to the idea that what is is and what is was perfect, I was able to practice reserving judgment, which truly changed my perspective on life. Many times I would find myself hearing incredible information, which I would then file in my memory bank, reserving judgment until further validation appeared. Two friends who did not know each other guided me to get a psychic reading from a woman named Gladys who became my Spiritual guide. Studying with Gladys opened my eyes and heart to the unseen realms of reality.

Running alongside with my new education in spirituality was a deep fascination with my own garden. I loved playing in my garden with different combinations of plant material. In time my garden grew into amazing proportions. The garden was thriving with the help of the fairies. People would stop in front of the garden and drink in the beauty and the energy. Soon I had a little garden business going. Just when my garden business was beginning to take off, it was time to take our second journey.

One of the many gifts of taking these journeys in our early thirties was that we stepped out of what was considered 'normal' for our age group and stepped into retirement mode. We had endless hours being in nature, living in National and State parks. We spent one month in each state of the western United States, and some time in western Canada, then we returned to Mexico. After 18 months we returned home. It became clear to me before we left on this second trip that my two great passions were gardening and spirituality. Spending so much time in nature was imprinting me with the knowledge for my future career. Another gift during the second trip was that we were meeting spiritually like-minded people, which certainly confirmed for me many of the teachings that I had received from my spiritual teacher, Gladys.

Upon our return to the reality of earning a living, I was blessed with a job of designing and planting flower gardens for the clients of an upscale nursery close to home. The experience gave me the knowledge I needed to start my own business. My husband taught himself to be a contractor, building and re-modeling homes, so we created Cooper and Cooper Homes and Gardens as our combined business. We were both fortunate to acquire all our work through referrals.

Working with nature and continuing my spiritual quest at the same time I became more aware of the nature spirits and how they contributed to the magic that was happening in the gardens that we created together. I am not able to see nature spirits with my physical eyes but I can feel them and sometimes I experience flickering movement around me. The other sensation that would alert me to their presence was a burning feeling in the palms of my hands. I would and still do always acknowledge them and thank them for their loving support.

"They love co-creating with humans!"

I came to realize that the nature spirits came with me into the new gardens that I was called in to create, staying until all the plants were happy. Not only was the garden activated but the land as well. The whole environment and the people living in and visiting the gardens received a healing. People walking by would stop to absorb the beauty and be filled by the lovely energy. I am so very grateful to be bringing such beauty into the lives of the people who call me into their gardens.

Twenty-five years of intense focus around gardening and spiritual studies have brought me to an ever-expanded awareness and a new location to live. I was given the guidance to leave California and I am now living in Arizona. I basically walked away from my flourishing garden business to find myself living on two acres in the country close to Sedona. Landing here has been an interesting experience in learning how to be still and to surrender into my new life. The last two years have given me the opening to create in a new way.

I have been told more than once through psychic readings that I am to write books as I have much information to share. The idea came to me to write about the fairy realm along with the thought to photograph the gardens that I have done, asking the fairies to show up in the pictures.

I was called back to California to do some gardens so I invited one of the four photographers who have contributed to finding fairies to join me. Upon entering one of my recently completed gardens we got still and meditated, calling the fairies in, asking them to please support us in showing themselves. We would open up our senses and be drawn to possible locations in the garden and then shot multiples of digital photos. We were absolutely delighted when we found our first fairy. We found that after each garden shoot that our energy levels were depleted. The answer came to me that the nature spirits exist in a higher frequency plane and for them to show themselves they had to draw from our energy field or ectoplasm.

In all my years of research with the fairy realm I have never seen actual photos of them that were not suspicious in some way. I have come across many drawings of nature spirits that have been psychically seen by others, and I have seen many photos of shimmering orbs. One of my most treasured books on the subject of fairies that my teacher Gladys gave me many years ago is called "A True Fairy Tale" by Daphne Charters. Daphne had an ongoing communication and friendship with the fairies in her garden. They described their environment, their work and their relationships. Daphne documented these encounters in her book. To my knowledge this is no longer in print, but there is a volume of Daphne's collected Fairy manuscripts compiled by Michael Pilarski called "Forty Years with the Fairies". It is printed by R.J. Stewart Books in Arcata, Ca.

Itallan Cypress gnome faces in their seed buds.

In the Beginning –

What could you share about the origin of the fairies?

It began as with all things in the beginning with the thought of the Infinite Creator. The fairies and nature spirits were set in place to be the work force of nature. They are an aspect of the Angelic realm and are responsible for all that we see around us on our beautiful Mother Earth. Their job of holding the form of nature is one of service to the whole and is what they strive to create through Divine Will. Their course of evolution is strictly adhered to and is guided by the higher ups in the Angelic realm. The entire population of this realm is in service to the greater whole of evolution on this planet. They are the worker bees providing substance to the world around us providing the living force to the land. As in many fairy tales they show up when we humans need a lift or when we feel lost or confused. They act as a guiding light to show us the way. They plug into our thought fields giving us a push in a direction needed in the moment.

It often appears to us that they transport us into a place of fantasy, a place where anything is possible. Could it be that they help us to remember a time when we were all playing together in a world filled with magic? Remember the unicorns, the dragons and the mer people. Where have they gone? I believe that they exist still but on another plane of demonstration.

Tree Beard is my name and I am so very pleased to show myself to you. We spire towards the sky, bringing energies from the celestial realms, anchoring them into the earth through our roots. We communicate with all the other trees via our root systems. The wind brings us the joy of movement. It also provides a clearing and cleansing of our leaves and branches. We really appreciate it when our human family nurtures and admires our beauty and shares love.

They disappeared due to the density of our human thoughts and emotions.

Let us invite them back by opening our hearts and minds to them. We can do this by letting go of our fears and using our imagination, seeing a world filled with infinite possibilities.

"We are here to tell you of our origin and more."

It was a time of true magic on Earth when all was being created. We came into being then and have served through all time since the creation of our Mother Earth. The land and sea were sparkling with the light of many colors and we drew from that energy to enhance our creations. Our delight at the beauty around us was amazing. We watched as the many varieties of life appeared on the planet and we took to our new responsibilities gladly. Nurturing baby animals being born, coaxing the seeds forming into plants and flowers was our duty. All was precious to us and still is. Pulsing energy into our charges with love is the way we work. Some humans were able to see glimpses of us and so the stories were shared from generation to generation. Some folks wrote down the stories turning them into fairy tales. Many children have seen us through time but as they got older dismissed their visions as fantasy. Well, fantasy is also real on a less tangible basis.

Years ago I happened upon a movie called "My Dinner with Andre". Two men were sitting at dinner sharing their adventures. One of them started talking about a place called Findhorn in the north of Scotland. I became keenly interested as the subject involved co-creating with the Nature Spirits.

Peter and Eileen Caddy, spiritually awake individuals, found themselves destitute after losing their jobs. They moved with their children to a trailer park near the end of a desolate spit of land in northern Scotland called Findhorn. Needing to supplement their diet they decided to grow a garden. Since they had no experience in the matter they called in the fairies of their land asking for help. In time, with the aid of the Nature Spirits, they produced large and abundant fruits and vegetables. Soon they were selling their harvests. Word spread about their experiences and people began to show up from all parts of the world. Peter and Eileen wrote books on their experiences and later developed a community where individuals could come and live communally.

After reading all their books I decided that one day I would visit Findhorn. Eighteen years later, with many years of co- creating with the Nature Spirits in the gardens I created, I decided to travel to Findhorn. My intention was to find out if the energy there was similar to the energy flowing in my gardens. Outsiders can enter the Findhorn community by signing up for their "Experience Week". I found myself with a group of 20 people from all parts of the world. Our guides were two members of the Findhorn community. Everyone that enters the community has to work. We were each given the choice as to what we wanted to spend our time doing. The options included service on the hotel where we stayed, preparing the food, or working in the gardens. I chose to work in the original garden where The Caddy's lived. It was a pleasure and a delight to find that the energy was the same.

The Findhorn River was one of the places that we visited. We were driven in one of their small white buses named after a popular flower, Rose. After a 45 minute drive we were dropped into the most magical fairy filled forest surrounded by ancient trees and spongy moss filled earth. Imbedded with peat flows, The Findhorn River flows dark brown in color and rages through the forest. We were asked to find a quiet place to meditate and commune with nature. Much to my surprise I found myself having a telepathic conversation with Pan, one of the Gods of Nature. He shared with me how pleased he was to connect and honored the work that I was doing with the nature spirits.

Much to my delight, Pan recently entered my thought fields. We set up a dialog of questions from me and answers from him. Here is some of the information that he shared.

Conversations with Pan, a God of Nature

Q. How do the fairies, gnomes, devas, elves and you set up your daytime activities? Do you sleep at night?

A. *Yes. We sleep just like humans. At day break we rise, then go about finishing the task of the day before. If we have a new project we focus on that.*

Q. Who guides you as to what to work on?

A. *I am in communication with Lord Kuthumi who is in charge of all the Nature Spirits. We discuss the overall goings on and I depend upon him for information as to upgrading energy shifts and how to best integrate the energies while continuing service upon Mother Earth.*

We are constantly balancing and recording, keeping everything moving in a beneficial direction. Our relationship is based on love and focused commitment toward ascension. Like you we are moving in the same cosmic direction.

Each being has a certain skill set which they do every day. The fairies draw the color from the atmosphere working on a particular plant bringing the green to the leaves and the brown to the branches and the color to the flowers. They stay with their particular plant until it completes its cycle. The gnomes work with the soil bringing the nutrients to the roots of the plants. The devas oversee a particular region of nature. They hold the overview working with the land as well as the air and water spirits.

Q. And what do you do, Pan?

A. *I am in communication with all of these beings on a daily basis adding my energy where needed. I am also listening to the humans balancing and drawing the vital energies where needed. We all work together for the best possible outcome for earth and humanity and ourselves. We are so delighted when our creations turn out splendidly.*

Q. Do you pull from human thought forms?

A. *Most definitely! We especially like working with humans who are aware of us and love to co-create such as yourself. We go about our daily business but have so much more fun when a human is involved.*

Q. Where do you rest at night?

A. *We have our own places that we create usually in nature.*

Q. What do they look like?

A. *They can be under the leaves and bushes and trees.*

We like places where we feel protected from the elements. We form a cocoon made up of light fibers around us when we are sleeping. The fibers are alive and will warn us of any danger. They are like a cloak we shed when we awake reforming them when needed.

Q. Do you dream?

A. *Yes we do. Like you we move out of our bodies when we sleep and astral travel.*

Q. How long do the fairies live?

A. *The fairies live on the earth plane until they have completed or mastered the tasks they came here to accomplish. That can be anywhere from 50 to 150 years of earth time. It is an evolutionary process for them. At times they stay even longer.*

Q. Do you age?

A. *No we just stay till we are done and then return to Source to revitalize and set up our next evolution.*

Q. What do the house fairies focus upon in their work?

A. *Their job is to hold the form of the building and to keep everything in place. They are directing the colors, the air, the fire and water that are awake and moving. They delight in the beautiful objects that you choose in* your surroundings. They also keep tabs on your energy field by lifting your spirits when you feel down. They keep you safe by blocking negative energies from entering. The higher your vibration, the higher theirs.

Q. What can we humans do to make them happy?

A. Acknowledge them and thank them for their support by blessing the water, the air and the fire whenever you use them. You can also leave small gifts for them. They really like sparkling things and sweets. Being aware of them makes them happy.

Q. Can you tell me about the healing nature spirits?

A. We are constantly searching for the discordant energy streams. When we become aware of them we send loving rainbow light into them until we see the streaming glowing again. We hold the vision, pumping energy until the stream stabilizes. That is how we heal all things and beings. There are times when the beings are too far gone and need to release their physical hold on their form. Areas are cleansed through weather as in rain, wind, snow, fire and earth movement. Mother Earth directs her nature spirits to undo stuck energy in this way. Negative human thought forms are constantly creating chaos. It is most important that all of you humans be conscious as to where your thoughts are focused as they affect a broad spectrum of your outer and inner reality. When you are able to embrace a peaceful inner world your outer world will reflect the same. Know this to be a most powerful truth.

Each time you have a negative thought instantly change it to a positive loving thought and eventually all your thoughts will be harmonious. Your life will flow with ease and grace. Imagine if every person were to accomplish this simple act, there would be no more violent nature to contend with.

In these times of seeming chaos, look to the beauty, the joy, and the love that surrounds you in gratitude.

See the magic everywhere.

Q. Can you speak of the will of Mother Earth and her minions of nature spirit helpers?

A. Mother Earth has made her shift to the next dimensional level and eagerly awaits her full light consciousness. This process can only occur one step at a time. As she moves, so do the rest of us. Be aware that all is happening at an accelerated rate. Our intention is to assist by making sure that evolution flows smoothly. What we endeavor to help create is a seamless transition from density to light. As we move so does the rest of the Universe.

In these times of seeming chaos, look to the beauty, the joy, and the love that surrounds you in gratitude. See the magic everywhere. Cast away your fears and doubts and imagine a world as you would like to see it evolve. We are all in this together. With each of us doing our part, anything is possible. Know that you are loved beyond measure.

Owl being embedded in a tree trunk.

Who are Nature Spirits & what are their functions?

Everything that we see is being held in form by a Nature Spirit.

Nature Spirits are part of the lineage of the Angelic realm. Known as Ra-Arus, Hiarus, Aspirites, Faralles, Fairies, Devas, Gnomes, Undines, Farisilles, Wallotes and more. They operate on a different dimension than ours, vibrating at a higher frequency that being the reason that most of us are not able to see them with our physical eyes. They serve by infusing power from Source into their intended focus, creating the forms that we observe in nature. Everything that we see is being held in form by a Nature Spirit. They start out in a very rudimentary form working in groups. Once they master a particular focus they return to the astral realm to rest until they are ready for their next cycle of creativity. Their evolutionary process of coming to Earth then returning to the astral realm elevates their responsibilities, their form and their consciousness. They evolve according to a specific plan and live their lives accordingly. Here on Earth humans have been gifted with free will. The Angelic realm operates within Divine will.

According to the Deva Marusis in Daphne Charters book "A True Fairy Tale", the lowest forms of fairy life are known as **Rudimes** who have little intelligence. They move around like insects stimulating the plant life and do not absorb and give out power. Their life span is short and they are approximately 1/8" tall.

Next they show up as **Unitis** experiencing individual consciousness. They are capable of absorbing and giving power on a limited basis. It takes many of them to keep a small patch of grass alive. They are on Earth for one year and are ½" in height.

Their next evolution as **Minutes** find them still working in groups to produce enough power to stimulate the plants growth. They are between one and two inches tall and live on Earth for five years. With each evolution they return to the Astral realm for periods of rest and growth until it is time for their return to Earth. At this stage they begin making decisions for themselves.

Succulent gnome smiling

As **Nomenes** or **Gnomes**, their work is with the earth, the trees and the roots. They stay for 25years and are able to separate their work from their play. They love playing games and copying the actions and objects which they observe.

The next stages are the **Elfines** or **elves** and **brownies**. They are found in the wild lands away from mankind. Their work is guiding the Minutes and Unitis, creating barriers of power, harnessing their energy and exhaling it out. Elves are happy and enjoy their recreation. They vary in size from a few inches to one foot in height. They stay on Earth for about fifty years then return to the Astral for a thousand years changing into fairies.

Fares or **Fairies** are more developed mentally and for the first time experience suffering. They get to choose their work with the vegetable or mineral kingdoms or with man through thought forms in healing the sick. They can learn to control the elements of fire, water or air as well as study color composition which is an important part of life on Earth. They guide the appropriate colors from the atmosphere to the individual flowers, all plants and minerals, infusing them with power.

Undinis are the inland water fairies and live on Earth for two hundred years. Their job is to guide the water from its source along its natural route infusing it with power until it reaches the ocean where the Nerenes take charge of the oceans. The Nerenes job is much more strenuous as great concentration is necessary when the sea is rough.

Baby face in the center of the Daffodil showing herself reaching for the sunlight

The fairies of the air are known as **Wallotes** and **Arienes**. They control the wind, and as there are waterways, there are air channels which they infuse with power to maintain the balance in the atmosphere.

Farisilles and **Shallores** are the nature spirits of fire. Fire is the most difficult element to direct. Fire and air fairies work together to direct the energies for a benevolent outcome. Without these beings we could not start a fire. Fire is the great destroyer and from it new creation arises.

Fairies who have mastered all aspects of experience on the Earth plane can choose to become **Faralles**.

It is important to give gratitude to these devoted, loving beings for their ongoing work of infusing power into the forms of nature.

Faralles are the teachers and leaders of the lesser nature spirits and take command when an important operation is to take place. Their job is to train other leaders in their particular focus.

Above the Faralles are the **Aspirites** who carry out the plans when fire, air, water or disease have gotten out of control. Their constant vigilance combined with their mental strength support nature to come into balance.

Hiarrus are the governors who make the plans for the Aspirites to follow. They are the creators of all great ideas for the ones below them to bring into form.

The **Ra-Arus** in the Fairy evolution are as the Archangels of Man. They are the leaders that add power and inspiration to all so that their purpose is fulfilled.

With this basic understanding of the journey of the Nature Spirits evolution from the Deva Marusis, it is important, in my opinion, to give gratitude to these devoted loving beings for their ongoing work of infusing power into the forms of nature that we witness on a daily basis in the world that we share.

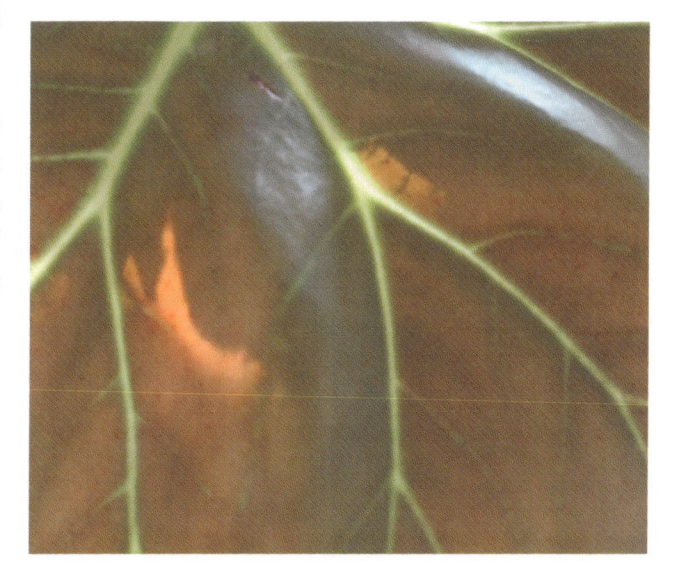

Begonia leaf gnome sharing his face in silver

I am known as Cynthia and I am the fairy in charge of this newly planted garden. I oversee the elementals and fairies in this space to ensure the success of all the new plant beings. Once everyone is established I move to a new garden that has been planted. I have been following you around for many years Linda and have always been by your side. Your gardens have been a pleasure to behold and to live in.

Thank you, Cynthia, for your support and appreciation.

Flower faces aplenty

Daffodil bud emerging
showing its baby face

Find the daffodil bud fairy face and notice
the gnome being in the red rock

Fairy Princess

Sunset fairy princess being showing herself

My name is Princess and my work involves capturing the light from the sun and infusing the plants with color and energy. I float around under the foliage transferring energy to the leaves and flowers, as they require. When the sun is up I am working. When the sun sets I am resting by floating in the air. I emit color and light through my crown for the plants to absorb.

Thank you, for sharing with us, Princess.

Gnomes

Rock beings known as gnomes surround us and want us to be aware of them by showing their images for us to acknowledge. They are delighted when we see them.

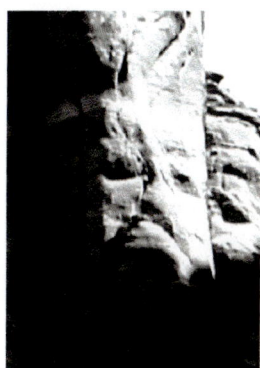

An aspect of Cathedral Rock in Sedona, Arizona. This place is one of the many vortexes around Sedona and is considered the only feminine vortex. I have found the energy of the center to feel viscous verses electromagnetic. See the many faces as well as the sentient beings standing together. We are witness to them and they to us.

Gnome keeper of the water flow smiling with us.

Flying dragon how did you come to be caught in the red rock?

I am here by the grace of the fairies. They wanted you to see the magic of my realm of transformation through fire. We exist in a dimension close to yours but not visible to your eye. We hope that in the near future you will be able to see us again. We so look forward to playing together. All you need do is believe that it is possible.

Happy Watcher Of The Valley

Sedona rock beings showing their beautiful selves.

We are the watchers of this valley. Our responsibility is to remind you that we are alive by sharing our faces with you. As you see us, we see you, and smile.

Rock gnome peeking through spider web

"The crystals have come as messengers and teachers in our search for understanding. They are here to support the reconnection to heritage and bring us back into harmony.

Merging with the frequency of a particular crystal matches the energetic band and transfers information on a cellular level to bring conscious change into our lives."

Crystals

I am the keeper of this crystal. My name is Harvey and I have been sharing myself in lightness for eons. I am holding the crystalline information connecting to all through the crystalline grid of Mother Earth. Our living library is open to all to share. Meditate with me and I will impart my wisdom. We have come to remind you of your galactic ancestry. We hold space in the crystalline form to show you the way home. Focus on my image and you will remember. Know that you are loved beyond measure and that we are here to support you through your transition into full consciousness. Some of us are able to move in and out of the crystalline structure as there are others holding the form.

The other realm where fairies and gnomes have shown themselves is inside the crystals that I have been collecting for many years. The mineral kingdom is here to support greater awareness towards personal power. The crystals have come as messengers and teachers in our search for understanding. They are here to support the reconnection to heritage and bring us back into harmony. Merging with the frequency of a particular crystal matches the energetic band and transfers information on a cellular level to bring conscious change into our lives. They are here to support the balancing of the divine masculine and feminine energies within each one of us. It is the mineral kingdom that supports all life on our beautiful planet by making up the soil, which feeds the plants, the animals and the water and the humans. The minerals of the earth are all connected energetically in communication with one another and Mother Earth.

Visiting gem shows on a regular basis has opened up a world of fascination. The miners and vendors selling their stones shared much of their knowledge which enhanced my awareness. This experience finds me with a vast collection of minerals from all over the world. At first I was interested mostly in the rough stones until I was introduced to the gem quality stones. Now I have all manner of minerals living with me in my home. Having these beings living with me has certainly raised the vibration in my environment. People who come for a visit at first are stunned by the beauty and the energy that the minerals emit.

Crystals have been a part of my life for many years. I was introduced to them upon my first visit to the Tucson Gem and Mineral show. The eye opening experience led me into a deep study of the minerals as well as their metaphysical properties. The fluorite octahedrons were my first fixation. Mined in Illinois they come in varying colors of pastel shades of yellow, blue, violet and clear. The miners would cleave them in the shape of an octahedron. The octahedron is in the shape of a pyramid going in both directions indicating as above so below. Fluorite has the frequency to assist in developing self discipline. As I was in the beginning stages of waking up spiritually this stone was perfect for me. I would use it in my meditations by holding onto it in my left hand then put my intention upon that which I wanted to change in my life. The left hand is considered the receiving side and the right hand is considered the sending. I found the effect soothing and helpful. When my journey was complete with fluorite I was led to whatever was to serve me next.

People who come for a visit at first are stunned by the beauty and the energy that the crystals emit. After being surrounded by the crystals they receive a healing and feel uplifted.

My landscape design ability served me in coming up with a way to display the crystals into what I call Crystal Scapes. Placing them in and around homes and gardens in combinations of color, shape, and height is a delight to the eye. Energetically they are a pleasure to live with and have the ability to support well being on all levels.

Many of the beings in the crystals in my home can be experienced in the photographs below. Use your imagination to witness the magic.

Find the robed being holding and directing a staff working the magic.

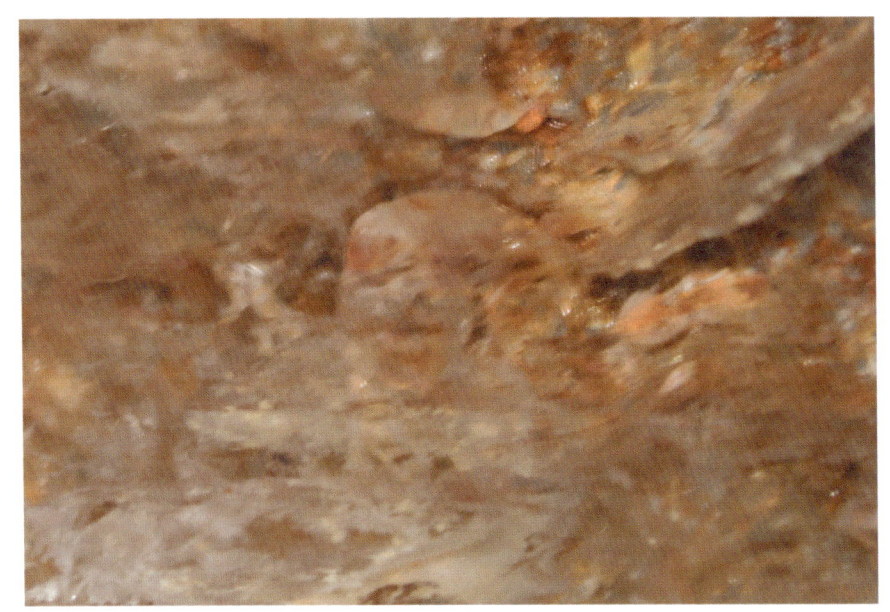

The cave of the gnomes sharing their magical selves for our viewing

Happy baby faces in a crystal slab

We live in a crystal in your home and have been holding the form of this crystal for eons of time. We are in constant communication with all the other crystal gnome beings on the planet. Our purpose is to telegraph information, keeping it flowing. Think of us as a living library that can be accessed at anytime. We hold the history and moment-to-moment information of our Earth mother. This information is constantly transmitted into the galaxy as we are sharing our condition with the rest of the planets and the sun in our solar system. We are so pleased that you have seen me and that we are communicating. We want you to see us and know about our purpose.

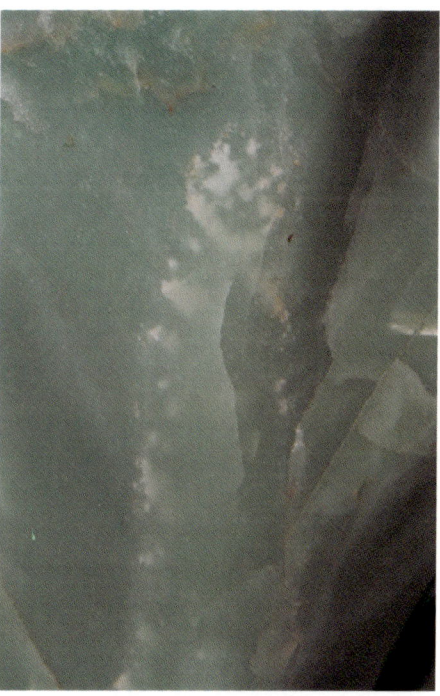

Crystal fairy queen showing herself in a green Aventurine known as a stone of prosperity with a strong connection to the Devic Kingdom.

Crystal Gnome

That which we term the Devic Kingdom, are essentially fragmental aspect of the elemental, mineral and plant kingdom that find conscious dynamic expression through vehicles of electromagnetic energy. Some Devic forms are more advanced than others. Those of the Fae or Fairy possess divine intelligence, whilst others of the Devic realm are more like your animals, in terms of thought patterns and group consciousness. Not all Devic forms are, what you may think of as positive or benevolent in nature. Some are consciousnesses sourced from electromagnetic fields and as such both positive and negative are required to balance the electrical spectrum you see. Some view mankind as brothers, others do not. Some are supremely loving, others are somewhat malicious, from your perspective. Yet both are electrical life forms in a manner of speaking.

All forms of life are sacred and it is appropriate as you grow in consciousness to attempt to understand the myriad of the great mystery.

Remember to grow in light requires eliminating fear, breaking the paradigm of limiting systems of belief.

Taken from (What is the Devic Kingdom channeling from Metatron through Earth Keeper. 11/1/2010

Notice his pointed ears, head and chin

Spirit

Spirit is my name. You are seeing my crown of light as well as my energy center of light where I transmit the frequencies supporting the form of this crystalline structure. I am in constant communication with all the crystalline beings in and on Mother Earth. We are sending and receiving pulses of information and energy at all times. It is a fluid process like breathing. When you focus upon one of us you are picking up frequencies that we are emitting. Consider it the language of light. We are thrilled to be working with you in this way and love showing ourselves with you.

Thank you, Spirit.

It is an honor to see you and know you and to be sharing in this way.

FAIRY PARTY: Imagine the world filled with fairy light

Queen of the Fairies

The queen of the fairies speaks of a time long past. In that life time there were big and dangerous problems for the group. The queen was not able to create the solution. It was a time of uncertainty on the planet. There was a war going on in the galaxy over who was going to control the earth. The dark forces were gathering power and overtaking not only the little people but the humans as well. Fear which was a new experience to all was overpowering all realms of reality. The fairies did not know what to do so they started shrinking out of sight. Their bodies became invisible to man. This was a very sad time for all as the two life streams were used to working together. As man became enveloped with fear all the other kingdoms had to protect themselves. The queen suggested to her fairy folk that they cloak themselves in invisibility. At first it was difficult as they had to develop the technique. They still did their source-directed duties of working with the elements but began to pull away from the humans. They continued to work with the animals by infusing them with ideas on how to operate and use their energy. The reason for the fall into fear rested with the new overlords of the earth. The overlords who had gained control of earth were of a mind to control the humans by instilling fear. They did not want the human beings to remember their God given gifts because the overlords were mostly interested in mining Mother Earth and using the humans to do the work. Of course mining would interfere with the fairies and gnomes territory as well. There were two factions of the overlords, one wanted to control and dominate, the other wanted to allow the humans to discover their spiritual side. As a result there developed a war between themselves. In the midst of it all fear predominated. The queen of the fairies was so stressed out about all the discordant energies, she directed her flock to lay low by going underground and stay out of sight. She felt sad that she could not turn the tide of fear into love and harmony so everyone did the best they could under the circumstances. As earth is a free will planet there was no recourse around asking the Angels and the Ascended Masters to intervene. All would have to run the time lines of separation till the light could take hold.

Thousands of years have had to pass in separation and now we find ourselves in a time of dimensional shifting where the Creator has mandated that light shall prevail and the dark ones must make a choice to come to the light or leave this plane of demonstration for an equally dense environment which will be provided for them to continue their dark stories. Now is the time for all kingdoms to lighten their burden by raising their vibration so that they can come into the light of a thousand years of peace and harmony and abundance on planet earth. So as we sit in this now time and place we see many changes occurring within ourselves and within others of our clans as well as many changes on our Mother Earth. It is time for the nature spirits to come out and play with the humans and for us all to live in harmony and visibility with one another.

The Wizard's Party

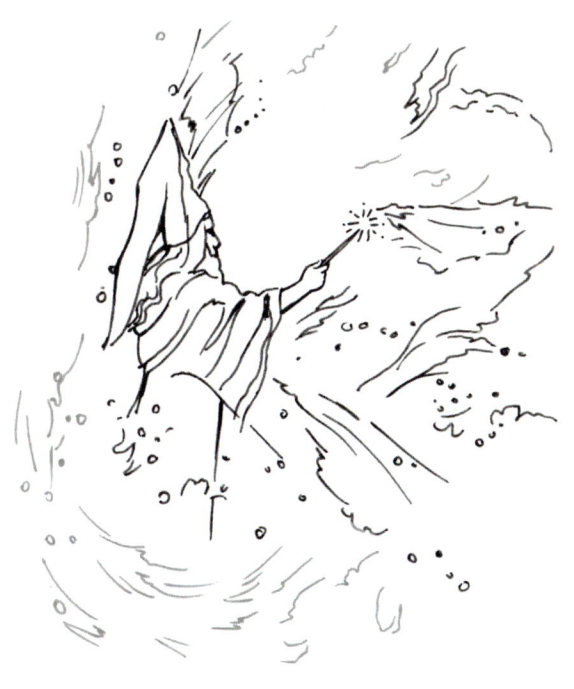

Filimina
of the Waterfall

I am Filimina of the waterfall and I love forming myself as you see me. I want to share my beautiful form with you at this time to show that we exist. We are with you always supporting the waters of the planet keeping them healthy and alive. Breathe in the light filled image and merge with the beauty of all that is around you. You are never alone.

Nature Spirits of the water known as Undinis are ever present in bringing us water by keeping it flowing and infusing the water with energy.

Nature Spirits of the Water

Fairy dancing in the waterfall

See her one arm reaching to the left and her other arm bent touching her eye. Her face looking straight out. They are constantly forming themselves into images that we can identify if we are fortunate enough to capture them.

Baby fairy playing with baby dragon

Find the many faces and beings frolicking in the waterfall.

A shimmering crystal emerging from a waterfall. Notice the face in the crystal.

Ghosts in the water

Cloud Beings

Nature Spirits of the air known as Wallotes and Arienes, as well as Sylphs, create cloud forms showing themselves in shapes that we can relate to such as human like faces, winged beings and animal figures to remind us of their presence. By opening our awareness and sending love we support their ever unfolding service to our atmosphere.

Look to the sky for Angelic shapes showing themselves to us letting us know that we are never alone

Angel cloud clearly showing itself. When you look closely at the face you can see the head with eyes, nose and mouth.

Find the cloud beings showing up
as faces for us to observe.

Angel being showing herself
at sunset in Arizona

Nature Spirits of Fire

Salamander Faces

When you light your fire we come into being. We are in the air waiting to be ignited by you. Our movements are fast and momentary. We transform matter into energy creating warmth for your comfort and pleasure.

Nature Spirits of fire called Farisilles, Shallores and salamanders playing with form and showing themselves as faces in the flames. Sometimes they can look quite scary. There is always a fire spirit present when you ignite a flame. Their job is to give off the perfect amount of power to create the warmth that you require. Be sure to give thanks to them when your flame appears.

Cat face in the fire hiding in the flames

Goddess of the fire

Salamnder spirit reaching up. Notice his profile and his arms creating his shape

Dolphin fire being

Fire face with a pointed chin with goatee

After Thoughts

Having spent the last twenty-five years creating gardens for my clients in Southern California, with my enhanced spiritual awareness, the results have been truly magic. Time and again, I have witnessed and experienced such beauty working with the nature spirits. The gardens themselves are so alive and filled with light that both my clients as well as their land have been transformed.

Once a garden has been planted, I have found that it takes about two years for it to become established. Gardens need refurbishing with soil prep, perennials and annuals, every 6 months. A garden is a living organism that appreciates love and attention. When we acknowledge the support of the nature spirits, the continued result is amazing.

All of nature, including humans, respond to love!

Find the face in the wood of the gate then look beyond at the micro beings showing up as faces behind the gate. Once we open our awareness to them they show up magically everywhere.

The Nature Spirits have shared with me that they are ready and willing to co-create with us in love to support the journey of transformation at this time on planet Earth. When you look at the photos in this book that have been collected, be sure to keep an open mind, which will expand your awareness and gift you with a whole new way of seeing the beauty and magic that surrounds you daily.

We gratefully appreciate the Nature Spirits for showing themselves to us at this time and happily share our journey with all of you.

Blessings and Love,

Linda Shaylor Cooper

The raw original photographs have been cropped to size, enlarged, clarified through defogging and otherwise remain in their original state.

Our beautiful sun who sustains life on our planet showing its beingness.

Linda Shaylor Cooper Bio

Transplanted from Durban South Africa to Southern California at an early age Linda spent a good portion of her life in Laguna Beach California. In her early thirties she had the amazing opportunity to spend two and one half years with her husband traveling in a VW bus through Mexico, Guatemala, and the western states of the United States as well as parts of Canada. This time away from the normal pace of work, family and the pursuit of a career gifted her with the time to reflect about her life, absorb the beauty of nature and discover her passions. Her husband having had a successful career in the practice of law took a sabbatical for one year. After the year of freedom was over they returned to Laguna Beach knowing that their life had changed dramatically. No longer could they return to what was. They purchased an old school bus with the idea to transform it into their new and expanded vehicle for the second trip which lasted for eighteen months. Her husband got a job as a recreational vehicle mechanic with the stipulation that the bus could be built while he was working there. Linda developed a passion for gardening and soon found herself invited into others gardens to maintain them.

Having walked away from organized religion at an early age Linda found herself questioning life and its mysteries. She had the good fortune to meet her spiritual teacher soon after her return from the first year of traveling. Gladys opened her eyes to the unseen aspects of life which included the nature spirit realm. With her intense focus on gardening came the realization that the nature spirits were working with her as her gardens vibrated with a magical quality. She found herself working at an upscale nursery where she had the opportunity to create flower gardens for the clients of the nursery. After 3 years of working for the nursery, learning how to run a landscaping business, she and her husband who taught himself to be a contractor formed their own business called Cooper and Cooper Homes and Gardens. 25 years of creating magical gardens calling herself The Garden Fairy and co-creating with the nature spirits while continuing her education spiritually she found herself ready to create in a new way. Leaving her long time business in California she moved to a 2 acre ranch property near Sedona in the high desert. Leaving the hustle and bustle of Laguna Beach and her business to live in the country found her applying her spiritual knowledge to the test. To learn to be still and trust that her next focus of creativity would show up. From the place of stillness, watching the flowers in her garden open, came the idea to create in a new way through asking the nature spirits to show up in photographs and write about them. With her life long love of the fairy realm and the willingness to share them they agreed to show up in the photos for all to see.

Linda now lives on her land with her cat, Beauty, and her lovely daughter, Azure Rose, who shows up regularly while attending university in Arizona.

Invitation to "Embracing the Spirit of Nature"

Nature spirits, and fairies have become increasingly common topics. Embracing the Spirit of Nature will invite you into a world of magic few have experienced by sharing actual raw photography of fairies, gnomes, and more.

Embracing the Spirit of Nature will alter how people experience nature and how they directly impact the life of all of nature's elements. This experience is similar to that of Masaru Emoto's work, demonstrating the life force that is present in every drop of water. His book shows how words of love and compassion cause drops of water to form clear crystal shapes.

My book will draw attention to nature spirits that have likely never been seen before, yet which surround and support us in our daily life.

The primary audience includes the spiritual community, people who currently interact with the fairy realm, people who love fantasy and the realms of magic, those who are interested in gardening, those who love nature, and children of all ages.

This book offers a unique opportunity to view actual raw photography of nature spirits including dialogs with the nature spirits. It also offers ways to communicate and receive guidance from the Nature Spirits. I have had the great pleasure of not only experiencing the fairies but have been blessed with the opportunity to view them through my photography.

Resources

Fairy events

http://www.friendsofthetrees.net/fairycongress/photos.htm

Forty Years With the Fairies
written by Daphne Charters
compiled by Michael Pilarski

What is the Devic Kingdom ?
(channeling of Metatron by
Earthkeeper.com 11/1/2010)

The Awakened Earth @ Awakened Earth.com

The Crystal Ally Cards
by Naisha Ahsian
Heaven and Earth Publishing

www.earthkeeper.com
Photographers
    Linda Cooper
    Phil Benson
    Mary Zaranto
    Nita Seneca

Artists renderings by Katie Doka

CPSIA information can be obtained
at www.ICGtesting.com
Printed in the USA
258103LV00001B